Courageous Kids

MARY ANNING
BREAKS NEW GROUND
COURAGEOUS KID OF PALEONTOLOGY

by Carol Kim

illustrated by Mark Simmons

CAPSTONE PRESS
a capstone imprint

Published by Capstone Press, an imprint of Capstone
1710 Roe Crest Drive, North Mankato, Minnesota 56003
capstonepub.com

Library of Congress Cataloging-in-Publication data is available on the Library of Congress website.
ISBN 9781666334289 (hardcover)
ISBN 9781666334302 (paperback)
ISBN 9781666334296 (ebook PDF)

Summary: In 1811, while exploring the cliffs near Lyme Regis, England, 12-year-old Mary Anning made the find of a lifetime. There in the rocks was the skeleton of an *Ichthyosaurus*. Mary went on to have a long career finding and identifying new dinosaur fossils. However, her work often went unrecognized by male scientists, and she received little credit until long after her death. Learn how Mary Anning's important discoveries influenced the science of paleontology.

EDITOR
Aaron J. Sautter

ART DIRECTOR
Nathan Gassman

DESIGNER
Brann Garvey

MEDIA RESEARCHER
Morgan Walters

PRODUCTION SPECIALIST
Polly Fisher

Direct quotations appear in **bold italicized text** on the following pages:
Pages 15, 19, 21: from *The Fossil Hunter: Dinosaurs, Evolution, and the Woman Whose Discoveries Changed the World,* by Shelley Emling. New York: Palgrave Macmillan, 2009.
Pages 16, 23: from "Mary Anning" by Famous Scientists: The Art of Genius, https://www.famousscientists.org/mary-anning/
Page 18: from "Mary Anning" by Museum of the Earth: Profiles, https://www.museumoftheearth.org/daring-to-dig/bio/anning
Page 27: from "Ammonite: Who Was the Real Mary Anning?" by Roz Tappenden, *BBC News*, October 17, 2020, https://www.bbc.com/news/uk-england-dorset-54510746.
Page 28, top left: from "How a Poor Victorian Woman Became a Legendary Fossil Hunter," by Adrian Currie, *Independent*, November 11, 2018, https://www.independent.co.uk/news/science/mary-anning-fossils-palaeontology-lyme-regis-women-geology-statue-victorian-era-a8617936.html.
Page 28, top right: from "Most Influential Women in British Science History," The Royal Society, https://royalsociety.org/topics-policy/diversity-in-science/influential-british-women-science/.

TABLE OF CONTENTS

The Jurassic Coast

About 200 million years ago, a 96-mile (155-kilometer) stretch of coastline in the south of England was underwater. The ocean was filled with strange creatures such as ammonites and squidlike belemnites. Large reptiles also swam in the seas, such as ichthyosaurs and long-necked plesiosaurs.

Over time, the oceans retreated, and the seabed rose to become cliffs and beaches. Left behind were the fossilized bones of the sea creatures that lived there millions of years ago. This area is now known as the Jurassic Coast.

In the early 1800s, the science of paleontology, or the study of fossils, was in its early stages. The word *dinosaur* hadn't even been created yet.

Scientists were just beginning to discover the fossilized remains of creatures that no longer lived on Earth.

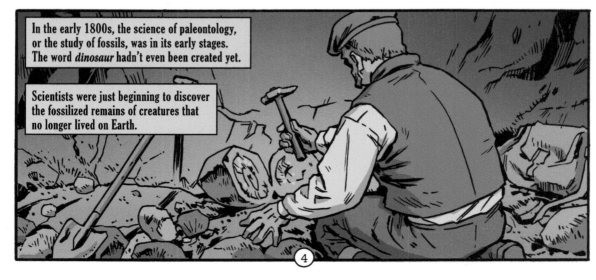

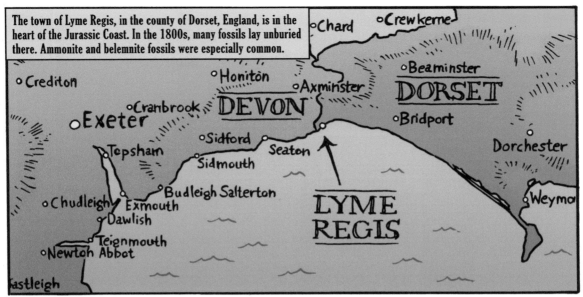

The town of Lyme Regis, in the county of Dorset, England, is in the heart of the Jurassic Coast. In the 1800s, many fossils lay unburied there. Ammonite and belemnite fossils were especially common.

During this time, almost all scientists were men. Most were from the upper social classes.

But one young girl would soon defy the odds. Her remarkable discoveries would have a huge impact on the world of paleontology.

In 1799, Richard and Molly Anning had a baby girl. They named her after her sister, who had died before Mary was born. Mary was a weak and sickly child.

We should name her Mary.

One day, when Mary was 15 months old, a family friend took her to a horse show. When a sudden rainstorm blew in, she held Mary while taking shelter under a tree with two other women.

Come, stay dry here out of the rain.

CRACK

But when lightning struck the tree, the three women were killed.

It's a miracle!

Incredibly, Mary was still breathing. Nearby witnesses rushed Mary home. Her parents gave her a warm bath, and Mary recovered.

Even more amazing, after the accident, Mary became a much livelier and healthier child. Her parents marveled at the change.

It's like she's a completely different child!

Mary's father was a carpenter and cabinet maker. But he preferred to spend his time searching the nearby beaches for fossils, or "curiosities" as they were often called.

As a young girl, Mary often went with her father to look for fossils. Richard made a small pick for her to use for digging at the cliffs. Mary's older brother, Joseph, often joined them. They sold the fossils to tourists who bought them as souvenirs and collectibles.

I've found something! Come see!"

Would you like to purchase a curiosity, sir?

Richard Anning's carpentry business didn't make much money. Selling fossils helped the family pay their bills.

Many women and girls, especially from poorer families, didn't get a formal education. Mary learned to read and write by going to Sunday School at their church.

Richard Anning died in 1810 from a combination of injuries in a fall and a disease called tuberculosis. Without his furniture business, the family became even poorer. Mary was only 11 years old. Her brother Joseph was 14.

It is just the three of us, now. What will become of us?

One day soon after her father's death, Mary went fossil hunting. She found a large ammonite. A woman saw Mary's discovery.

That is a beautiful curiosity! Would you be willing to sell it to me?

The woman gave Mary half a British crown for the fossil. That equals about $14 today. No one had ever paid her father so much money for a fossil! It was enough to buy her family food for an entire week.

Mary began to visit the beach and cliff area often. She hoped to find and sell more fossils to help her family.

Thank you kindly, ma'am!

People soon became interested in the odd shells and fossils of Lyme Regis. They were popular souvenirs. Some people even believed the objects carried special powers.

I've heard these can cure snakebites.

That's just an old wives' tale.

One day in 1811, Joseph came across an unusual fossil.

Joseph showed Mary what he had discovered.

It looks like the head of a giant crocodile!

It's about four feet long! We should look for the rest of the body. It must be around here somewhere.

After their father died, Joseph spent most of his time learning the upholstery business.

I don't have much time for fossils now that I'm working at Mr. Hale's shop. You'll have to be the one to find it, Mary.

Mary searched the area for the rest of the creature's body. Weeks passed, then months, but no skeleton was to be found.

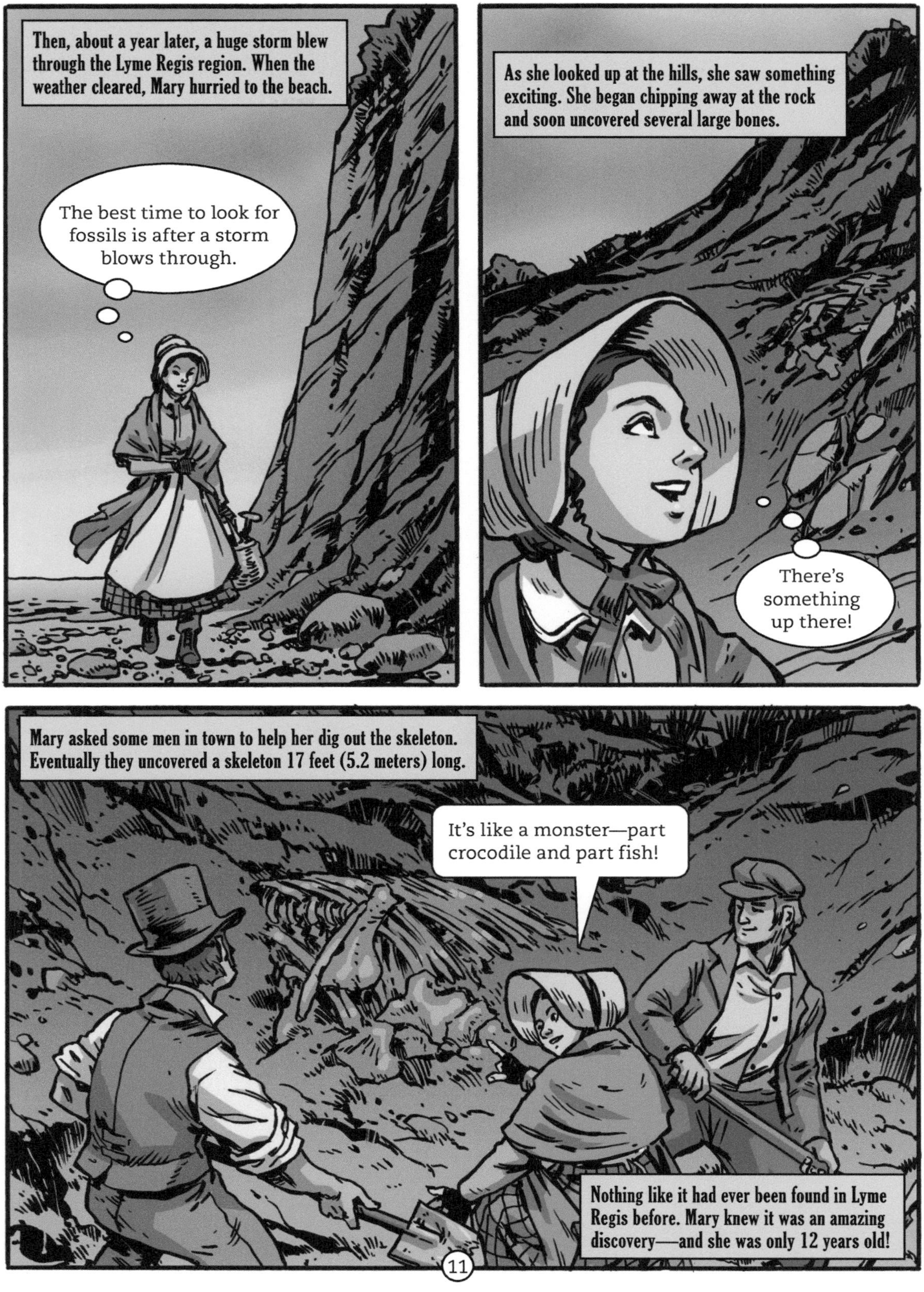

Then, about a year later, a huge storm blew through the Lyme Regis region. When the weather cleared, Mary hurried to the beach.
The best time to look for fossils is after a storm blows through.
As she looked up at the hills, she saw something exciting. She began chipping away at the rock and soon uncovered several large bones.
There's something up there!
Mary asked some men in town to help her dig out the skeleton. Eventually they uncovered a skeleton 17 feet (5.2 meters) long.
It's like a monster—part crocodile and part fish!
Nothing like it had ever been found in Lyme Regis before. Mary knew it was an amazing discovery—and she was only 12 years old!

Henry Hoste Henley was a wealthy landowner in Lyme Regis. He bought the fossil for £23, or about $2,600 in today's dollars.

This is enough to feed us for months!

News of Mary's find reached the scientific community in London. Scientists argued about what kind of creature the bones belonged to.

It's surely just the bones of a crocodile.

I think it must be from an unknown deep-sea fish.

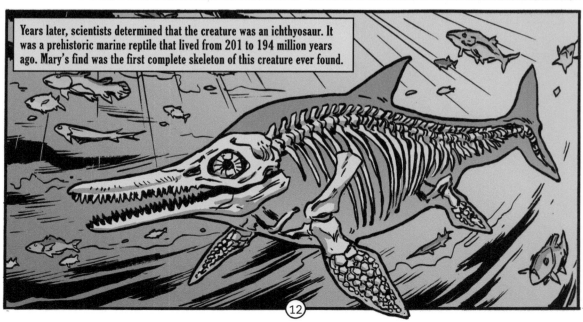

Years later, scientists determined that the creature was an ichthyosaur. It was a prehistoric marine reptile that lived from 201 to 194 million years ago. Mary's find was the first complete skeleton of this creature ever found.

Excited by discovering the skeleton, Mary threw herself into fossil hunting. Sometimes Joseph joined her, as well as Henry de la Beche, a young man around Joseph's age. Henry lived in Lyme Regis and was also very interested in fossils.

Between 1815 and 1819, Mary found several more complete ichthyosaur fossils.

When she was a young woman, Mary got a dog, whom she named Tray. He became a loyal and helpful companion.

I'll need to get some help to finish this.

Stay here, Tray, and guard the spot. This way I'll know where to find it again.

RUFF!

Good boy, Tray!

In 1818, Lt. Col. Thomas James Birch, a fossil collector, came to Lyme Regis. He had heard about Mary and her discoveries. He became a regular visitor and bought many fossils.

This will be a great piece to add to my collection!

A year later, when Mary was 20 years old, she found a nearly complete ichthyosaur skeleton. Birch bought it from her. It would be the last major sale Mary would make for some time.

The following year, Mary did not find any major fossils. By 1820, the family was running out of money.

We have to sell this furniture to pay next month's rent.

When Birch visited the Annings, he saw how they were struggling.

Mary hasn't found anything remarkable for a year. We are becoming quite desperate.

It isn't right that you are in this terrible situation.

Birch decided to sell his fossil collection and use the money to help the Annings. In a letter to his friend, geologist Gideon Mantell, Birch wrote:

I am going to sell my collection for the benefit of the poor woman Molly and her son Joseph and daughter Mary . . . I may never again possess what I am about to part with; yet in doing it I shall have the satisfaction of knowing that the money will be well applied.

Birch's fossil collection brought in £400. Today that would equal nearly $54,000. He gave it all to the Annings. It was enough for them to live comfortably for many years.

In 1823, at age 24, Mary made one of her most important discoveries. She found the first complete skeleton of a plesiosaur, another prehistoric sea creature.

My goodness, Tray! I've never seen anything like this!

I've seen bones like these before.

Nonsense! I don't believe this is a real creature.

The animal had an unusually long neck and small head. Some scientists, including the famous Georges Cuvier, often called "the father of paleontology," thought it was a fake.

The fossil was brought to the Geological Society of London. Some scientists didn't think any creature could have such a long neck. Others argued that the skeleton matched fossils from other parts of England. Mary was not invited to attend.

Mary's reputation as a fossil expert was in danger. But later, Cuvier studied the plesiosaur fossil and admitted he had made a mistake.

It is the most amazing creature ever discovered.

Mary soon became well-known for her discoveries. Scientists began to visit Lyme Regis to meet with her. One frequent visitor was William Buckland, a well-known geologist and paleontologist.

You have caused quite a stir with your plesiosaur, Mary! You are becoming quite well-known.

I'm happy to hear it. It's past time I received credit for my work.

Mary made another interesting discovery in 1826. Belemnite fossils were common in Lyme Regis. They were from squidlike creatures that lived 200 million years ago.

One day, Mary cut one open and noticed something inside. She showed the fossil to her friend and fellow collector Elizabeth Philpot.

This looks like an ink chamber, just like a squid.

Let's add some water to it.

It is ink! Look! It works quite well.

You could sell drawings made with the belemnite ink.

In 1828 Mary found another amazing fossil. It was unlike anything she had ever seen before.

It has wings with claws and a tail. It's like a flying lizard.

Mary had discovered a pterosaur, or "winged lizard."

William Buckland wrote about Mary's discovery. For the first time, he gave her the credit for finding it.

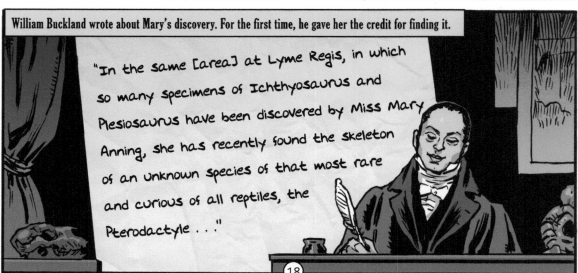

"In the same [area] at Lyme Regis, in which so many specimens of Ichthyosaurus and Plesiosaurus have been discovered by Miss Mary Anning, she has recently found the skeleton of an unknown species of that most rare and curious of all reptiles, the Pterodactyle . . ."

As time went on, Mary made several other major discoveries. In 1829, she found a more complete skeleton of a plesiosaur.

She wrote to William Buckland that "it is without exception the most beautiful fossil I have ever seen." She had discovered a new species of the marine reptile.

Mary later discovered a strange fossil. Its head looked like a shark's, and its body was flat with fins like a stingray.

It is a skeleton with a head like a pair of scissors.

It took several years for scientists to figure out that it was a kind of fish. It is now known as a chimaera, sometimes called a ghost shark.

Mary noticed some strange-looking stones in some of the ichthyosaur fossils she found. She broke some open and found bits of animal parts inside. She was one of the first to figure out what the stones were.

Why, these must be ancient fossilized poop!

Mary worked with William Buckland to study the fossilized poop. He later named the stones *coprolites*.

Mary's work helped scientists learn more about what prehistoric animals had eaten.

This is so interesting! This screw-shaped one could be from a fish whose guts are spiral-shaped.

And this one has bits of bones—probably from fish it had eaten.

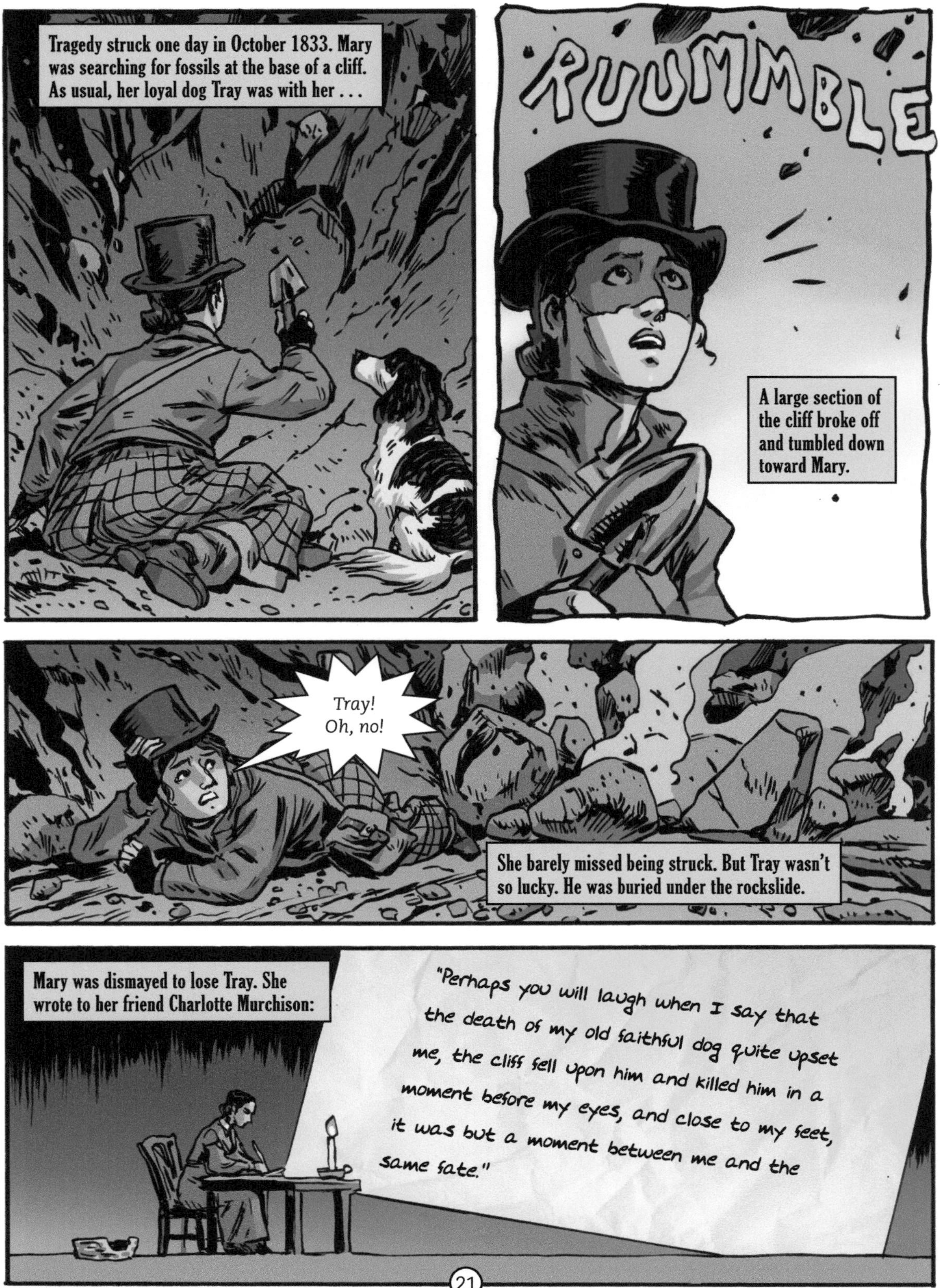
Tragedy struck one day in October 1833. Mary was searching for fossils at the base of a cliff. As usual, her loyal dog Tray was with her . . .
RUUMMBLE
A large section of the cliff broke off and tumbled down toward Mary.
Tray! Oh, no!
She barely missed being struck. But Tray wasn't so lucky. He was buried under the rockslide.
Mary was dismayed to lose Tray. She wrote to her friend Charlotte Murchison:
"Perhaps you will laugh when I say that the death of my old faithful dog quite upset me, the cliff fell upon him and killed him in a moment before my eyes, and close to my feet, it was but a moment between me and the same fate."

Many people were amazed by Mary. They didn't expect a young woman from a poor family and little education to know so much about fossils.

She worked hard not only at finding fossils, but also to learn all she could about them. She borrowed many books and taught herself anatomy.

Mary also learned geology, paleontology, and scientific illustration. She dissected fish to compare them to the fossils she discovered.

Why do you keep cutting open dead fish, Mary?

They're fascinating. I can learn so much by studying how they're made on the inside.

In spite of her discoveries, Mary was rarely given credit for her work. Because she was a woman, she wasn't allowed to become a member of the Geological Society of London.

NO WOMEN ALLOWED!!

GEOLOGICAL SOCIETY

Mary's discoveries were having a major impact on the field of paleontology. Her finds supported the theory of extinction, which scientists were just beginning to understand. Some did not accept it.

Cuvier is saying animals that once lived on Earth have vanished forever.

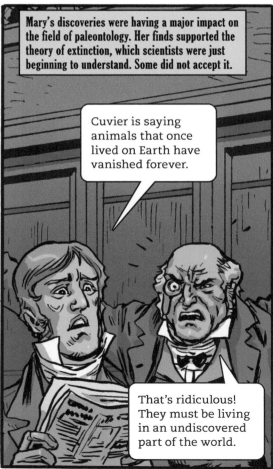

That's ridiculous! They must be living in an undiscovered part of the world.

Mary was frustrated that others were getting credit and rewards for her work.

Anna Maria Pinney, a friend of Mary's, wrote: *"She says the world has used her ill . . . these men of learning have sucked her brains, and made a great deal by publishing works, of which she furnished the contents, while she derived none of the advantages."*

WILLIAM BUCKLAND

Despite Mary's success at finding fossils, she and her family continued to struggle with money. It was getting harder for her to find buyers for her fossils.

When Mary's friend Henry de la Beche came for a visit, he had some news.

I've got a plan to help you and your mother, Mary.

Henry brought a painting he had made called *Duria Antiquior – A More Ancient Dorset*. It showed a scene of prehistoric life, including all the creatures Mary had found.

It's amazing!

Henry, your imagination has taken flight!

It includes all of the creatures you've discovered.

This was the first image ever made of what life may have looked like during prehistoric times. People were amazed at the scene. De la Beche had copies made of the painting and sold them. He sent the money to the Annings.

Could the oceans have really looked like this?

I must have a copy!

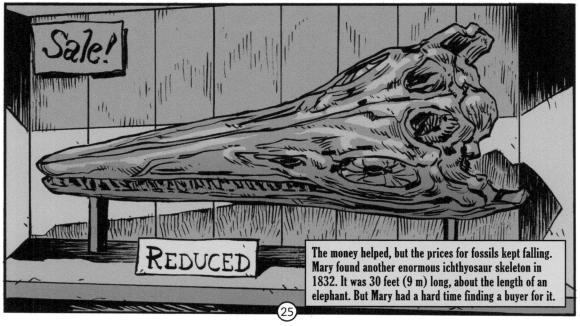

Sale!

REDUCED

The money helped, but the prices for fossils kept falling. Mary found another enormous ichthyosaur skeleton in 1832. It was 30 feet (9 m) long, about the length of an elephant. But Mary had a hard time finding a buyer for it.

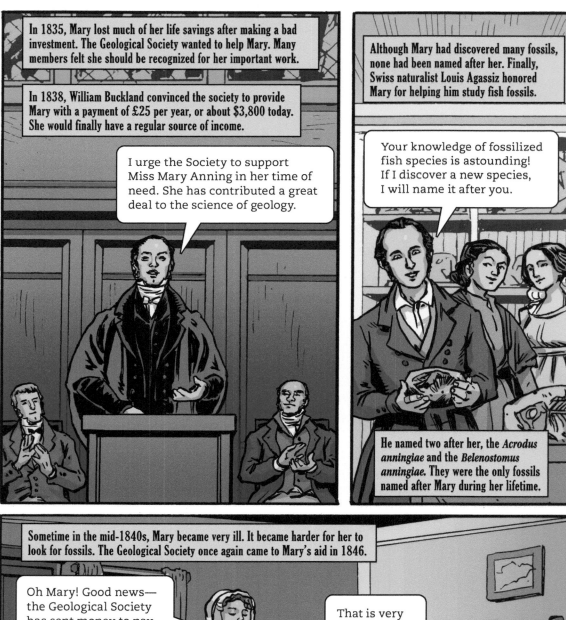

In 1835, Mary lost much of her life savings after making a bad investment. The Geological Society wanted to help Mary. Many members felt she should be recognized for her important work.

In 1838, William Buckland convinced the society to provide Mary with a payment of £25 per year, or about $3,800 today. She would finally have a regular source of income.

I urge the Society to support Miss Mary Anning in her time of need. She has contributed a great deal to the science of geology.

Although Mary had discovered many fossils, none had been named after her. Finally, Swiss naturalist Louis Agassiz honored Mary for helping him study fish fossils.

Your knowledge of fossilized fish species is astounding! If I discover a new species, I will name it after you.

He named two after her, the *Acrodus anningiae* and the *Belenostomus anningiae*. They were the only fossils named after Mary during her lifetime.

Sometime in the mid-1840s, Mary became very ill. It became harder for her to look for fossils. The Geological Society once again came to Mary's aid in 1846.

Oh Mary! Good news— the Geological Society has sent money to pay your medical bills.

That is very kind of them.

More public recognition for Mary soon followed. In 1846, a new Dorset County Museum opened.

In honor of her extraordinary contributions to the study of fossils, Mary Anning shall be the museum's first honorary member.

Mary died in 1847. She was just 47 years old.

People wanted to honor Mary. Members of her church, along with the Geological Society, dedicated a large stained glass window to her memory.

At that time Henry de la Beche was the president of the Geological Society. He wrote a speech in honor of Mary. It was the first ever written for a woman by the society.

[Mary Anning] contributed by her talents and untiring researches in no small degree to our knowledge.

Recognition at Last

Many people outside the scientific world didn't know about Mary or her work for many years. But that has begun to change. In 1995, British historian Hugh Torrens wrote that Mary was *"the greatest fossilist the world ever knew."*

In 2010, the Royal Society named Mary as the third most influential female scientist in British history.

They wrote: *"Anning's gender and social class prevented her from fully participating in the scientific community . . . and she did not always receive full credit for her contributions . . ."*

Mary Anning (1799–1847)

Caroline Herschel (1750–1848)

Mary Somerville (1780–1872)

More fossils were named in honor of Mary after her death. A plesiosaur was named as *Anningasaura* in 2012.

When a new species of ichthyosaur was discovered in Britain in 2015, it was named *Ichthyosaurus anningae.*

The Lyme Regis Museum was built on the site of Mary's fossil shop. A wing of the museum was dedicated to Mary's life in 2017.

In 2018 the Natural History Museum in London opened the Anning Rooms to honor Mary. Some of the fossils she found are displayed at the museum.

In 2018, 11-year-old Evie Swire began a successful campaign called "Mary Anning Rocks" to create a statue of Mary Anning in Lyme Regis. Work on the statue began in 2021.

Perhaps Mary's greatest legacy is found in the curiosity she inspires in thousands of children. Today many young fossil hunters visit Lyme Regis to look for fossils, just as Mary did 200 years ago.

GLOSSARY

ammonite (AM-uh-nyte)—a marine animal with a flat spiral shell that lived more than 66 million years ago

anatomy (uh-NA-tuh-mee)—the study of the body and how its parts are arranged and work together

belemnite (BEL-uhm-nyte)—a marine animal with a cone-shaped shell that lived more than 66 million years ago

extinction (ik-STINGK-shuhn)—the condition when all members of a species have died out, with no more of its kind left alive

geology (jee-AHL-uh-jee)—the study of minerals, rocks, and soil

Jurassic (juh-RAH-sik)—the period of geological history that ran from 200 to 145 million years ago

paleontology (pay-lee-uhn-TOL-uh-jee)—the study of fossils to learn and understand ancient forms of life

plesiosaur (PLEE-see-uh-sohr)—a large, swimming reptile that lived more than 80 million years ago

prehistoric (pree-hi-STOR-ik)—from a time before history was recorded

pterosaur (TEAR-uh-sohr)—a flying reptile related to dinosaurs that lived more than 66 million years ago

tuberculosis (tuh-BUHR-kyuh-low-sis)—a dangerous disease caused by bacteria that causes fever, weight loss, severe coughing, and sometimes death

READ MORE

Barnham, Kay. *History VIPs: Mary Anning*. London: Wayland Publishers, 2017.

Gibson, Karen Bush. *Paleontologists: With STEM Projects for Kids*. Junction, VT: Nomad Press, 2019.

Skeers, Linda. *Dinosaur Lady: The Daring Discoveries of Mary Anning, the First Paleontologist*. Naperville, IL: Sourcebooks Explore, 2020.

Vegara, Maria Isabel Sanchez. *Mary Anning*. London: Frances Lincoln Children's Books, 2021.

INTERNET SITES

Junior Paleontologist
nps.gov/subjects/fossils/junior-paleontologist.htm

Mary Anning Facts
natgeokids.com/uk/discover/history/general-history/mary-anning-facts/

Paleontology: The Big Dig
amnh.org/explore/ology/paleontology

INDEX

ABOUT THE AUTHOR

Carol Kim is the author of several fiction and nonfiction books for kids. She enjoys researching and uncovering little-known facts and sharing what she learns with young readers. Carol lives in Austin, Texas, with her family. Learn more about her and her latest books at her website, CarolKimBooks.com.